The
BABY BOOMER'S
Little Quiz Book

150 Questions To Prove You Really Grew Up Wearing Bell Bottoms

Beth Jones

BELL
BOTTOM
BOOKS

Kalamazoo, Michigan

The Baby Boomer's Little Quiz Book :
150 Questions To Prove You Really Grew Up Wearing Bell Bottoms

Published By: Bell Bottom Books
P.O. Box 555
Richland, MI 49083
1-800-955-4077
E-Mail: blbottombk@aol.com

All graphic images used in this book are from the "Incredible Image Pak", by T/Maker Company

ISBN 0-9656361-0-0

Additional copies of this book are available.
For your convenience, ordering information can be found at the back of this book.

Also available, "The Soccer Mom's Little Quiz Book - 101 Questions To Prove You Really Do Need Three Cappuccino's a Day"

Printed in the USA

Data Reproductions Corporation • Rochester Hills, Michigan

Proverbs 8:12

DEDICATION.

This book is dedicated to...

Waverly High School

Class of 1977

Lansing, Michigan

INTRODUCTION.

I wanted to marry Donny Osmond! I wanted to be Marsha Brady. I waited day after day for Gilligan, the Skipper too, the millionaire and his wife, the movie star, the professor and...Mary Ann to find a way to get off that island! I loved my Archie lunch box, bell bottoms, patchouli incense, hanging macrame plant holders, and The Carpenters on 8-track! I still know all the words to "I Think I Love You!"

I am a Baby Boomer, born in 1959, and this was my culture! If you are like me, born between 1946 and 1964 then we have a lot in common. We have our own history, our own code words, our own memories...all 76 million of us! We grew up in a time of unprecedented history...the 60's and the 70's. Our "group" changed the diaper industry, and the lunch box business. We put Coca-Cola and McDonald's on the map! Now, here we are in our 30's, 40's and 50's! We're busy dads and soccer moms. We're responsible for the recent "baby boomlet". Our old clothes are now cool again! We're driving mini-van's and sport utility vehicles. We're sending e-mail, talking on cellular phones, and surfing the web. We're on treadmills and in step-aerobic classes by the hordes and a few of us are even getting serious about anti-wrinkle creams. (In a few years, we'll change the diaper industry again, only this time they'll be called "Depends"!) We are the envied generation and we must never forget the things that made growing up as a Baby Boomer so fun!

Take a sentimental journey through this little quiz book and prove, to whoever cares, you **really** did wear bell bottoms - the first time they were popular!

HOW TO USE THIS BOOK.

Who are you? A "Die Hard Baby Boomer" or a "A Baby Boomer Wanna Be"? Take the Little Quiz and find out! We've listed 150 questions that cover numerous areas of our lives as Baby Boomers. From old TV shows, to fashion, to fads, to movies, and music...we tried to include a few questions from every area we could think of. Have fun!

1. **To Have Fun:** Get a pencil and take the "Little Quiz" yourself by filling in the blanks and following the prompts. The correct answers are in the back of the book.

2. **To Throw A Party:** Host a "Boomer" party and rent "The Brady Bunch Movie", "Mission Impossible" or "Flipper"...or any of the other remake movies we made famous...and have your whole party take the quiz.

3. **To Get A Date or Meet New Friends:** Carry this book with you at all times. Whenever you see someone who looks "babyboomerish" just begin quizzing them! What a great ice breaker!

4. **To Help Us Put Our Kids Through College:** Tell everyone you know about this book! Of course, they'll want their own copy and we have included convenient "Ordering Info" at the back of the book. Bless you!

5. **To Become Popular:** Give this book as a gift to all your Baby Boomer friends! It's a great Birthday present. Give it to everyone at your next class reunion and you will be the coolest person ever!

Footnote: This book is not based upon scientific study! Have fun!

To order more copies of this book please see the "Ordering Information" in the back of this book.

1

"Bell Bottoms and Hip _____"

2

Name these teen-age heart throbs.

"Donny_____"

"Davey_____"

"Bobby_____"

"David_____"

3

Things your mother said...

"Close the door, were you born in a _____."

"If you think it's my job to pick up after you,_____."

"Eat your food, there are children_____."

"Your room looks like a _____."

4

"Hey, Hey We're The_____!"

How long was "The Minnow's" tour?

_____

6

Name "George Jetson's"...

Wife_____

Son_____

Daughter_____

Dog_____

7

What were "P.F. Flyers" & "Red Ball Jets™"?

_____

8

"Danger! Danger! Go back Will Robinson!"
Who said that?

_____

Remember these slogans?

Where did you go if you wanted to have it your way?_____

Whose generation was it?_____

What did you deserve?_____

What did they want to teach the world to do?_____

10

Who is "Mrs. Beasley"?

_____

Remember these fads?

"Hoola_____"   "Lava_____"

"Platform_____"   "Pet_____"

"Mood_____"   "Pooca_____"

12

Can you whistle the "My Three Sons" theme song?
Go ahead!

In one of the popular "Dr. Seuss" books,
who didn't like "green eggs and ham"?

_____

14

Name the entire "Brady Bunch".

_____   _____

_____   _____

_____   _____

_____   _____

What "Led Zepellin" song played at the end
of every high school dance in the 70's?

_____

16

Name "Buffy" and "Jody's"...

Uncle_____

Older Sister_____

Caregiver_____

What are "Cooties" and "Cootie Spray"?

_____

18

Who lived at "345 Stonecave Road" and worked at the "Slaterock Gravel Company"?

_____

Which one wasn't a part of our childhood?

_____Cap'n Crunch®   _____Captain & Tennille

_____Captain Kangaroo   _____Captain Nemo

_____Captain Jean Luc Picard _____Captain Kirk

20

What does it mean to "pop a wheelie"?

_____

21

Name the 3 stars of the "Mod Squad".

_____

_____

_____

22

What group sang, "C'mon Get Happy" and "I Think I Love You"?

_____

During our childhood, what did most families do on Sunday nights?

_____

24

Name the characters of "The Dick Van Dyke Show".

_____ and _____ Petri

and their son_____

Can you sing the "McDonald's® Big Mac®" jingle?
Go ahead!

26

Who are "Colonel Mustard", "Professor Plum", and "Miss Scarlet"?

_____

"Kapow!", "Bash!", "Zap!" What show?

_____

28

Name "The Jackson 5".

_____   _____

_____   _____

_____

"I see Susie, I see Tommy, I see Michelle and I see you too! " What show?

_____

30

Name these 70's movies.

The luxury ocean liner that sunk_____

The highrise building on fire_____

The shark that kept everyone out of the water_____

The boxer who wouldn't be defeated_____

31

Who are "Wally Cleaver" and "Eddie Haskell"?

_____

32

What was a...

"Pixie"_____"

"Bee Hive"_____"

"Shag"_____"

"Billie Jo", "Betty Jo" and "Bobbie Jo", from "Petticoat Junction" lived in what town?

_____

34

Remember these songs?

What wouldn't spoil a whole bunch of girls?_____

Who was Jeremiah?_____

What was the lonliest number?_____

Who's house was a very fine house?_____

He wasn't heavy, what was he?_____

How did you "tie-dye" a t-shirt?

_____

_____

36

What did it mean if your parents had to call you by your first, middle, and last name?

_____

Can you describe "the" look? Mother's glare?_____

Can you remember "the" sound? Dad's snap?_____

37

Can you hum the "Bonanza" theme song?
Go ahead!

38

"Itsy, bitsy, teeny_____, _____,

_____, _____, _____." [11]

"And that's the way it is..."
Who said this every evening at 6:00p.m.?

_____

40

Can you say "Peace and Love" in "pig latin"?
Go ahead!

Did you know "jibberish"? A great code language
parents didn't understand? Let's hear it!

41

Describe the coolest outfit of your childhood!

_____

What were these fashions...

"Go-Go Boots & Fish Net Nylons"_____

"A Sizzler"_____

42

Remember "The Wild Kingdom"?

Who was the host?_____

Who was his assistant?_____
(Hint: "Watch now as he wrestles the wild alligator.")

Who was the major sponsor?_____

In the 70's, who were the two stars in the hit movie, "Grease"?

_____   _____

44

What really "cool" thing did we do to our bikes
with a deck of cards and clothes pins?

_____

Who are "Opie" and "Aunt Bee"?

_____

What town did they live in?

_____

46

Name everyone in "The Partridge Family".

_____   _____   _____

_____   _____   _____

Name these groups.

"The Jefferson_____"

"Three Dog_____"

"The Moody_____"

"Creedence_____"

48

Who is the mascot for "MAD® Magazine"?

_____

Can you sing the "Gilligan's Island" theme song?
Go ahead!

50

Name "Johnny Quest's"...

Best Friend_____

Dog_____

Remember these cars?

You were driving in your car and you saw a "Volkswagen Bug", what did you say and do to the person sitting next to you?

_____

Which car was not a part of our era?

_____"Gremlin" _____"Pacer" _____"Pinto" _____"Mini-Van"

_____"Matchbox" _____"Chitty-Chitty, Bang-Bang"

On "Green Acres"...

Who drove the junk truck?_____

What was the pig's name?_____

Name these popular singers from the 60's.

They sang, "Help Me Rhonda"_____

They sang, "Surf City"_____

They sang, "Blowin' in the Wind"_____

Their "Sold Out" album was a Billboard bestseller_____

54

What did "Thurston Howell" call "Mrs. Howell"?

_____

Did you play these outdoor games?

"Kick the_____"

"Einey-iney_____"

"Mother_____"

"Red Rover_____"

"Capture The _____"

"Dodge_____"

56

According to a movie from our era, if you love someone you never have to say your sorry. What movie?

_____

According to a popular poster from our era, if you love something what are you supposed to do with it?

_____

What character said, "Golly"?
(Hint: Pronounced - "gawawlly")

_____

58

What are...

"Teaberry", "Black Jack", "Clove", and "Beeman's"?_____

"Black Cow Sucker"_____

"Zots®"_____

Who are "Colonel Klink" and "Schultz"?

_____

60

In the game "Monopoly®", what color are "St. James Place", "Tennessee Avenue", and "New York Avenue"?

_____

"Hey kids, what time is it?" What show?

_____

62

Can you whistle "The Andy Griffith Show" theme song?
Do it!

Remember your metallic purple "Stingray"?
What was a "banana seat" and a "sissy bar"?

_____

64

Name the 3 boys on "My Three Sons".

_____

_____

_____

What female vocalists sang these songs?

"Stop In The Name of Love"_____

"I Am Woman Hear Me Roar"_____

"I Feel The Earth Move"_____

"Killing Me Softly"_____

66

What was unveiled at New York's World Fair on April 17, 1964? It only cost $2,368 and could accomodate a family of four!

_____

How much were the "Clampett's" really worth?

_____

What did "Jethro Bodine" call a swimming pool?

_____

68

Name "Popeye's"...

Girlfriend_____

Arch Rival_____

What did these characters want?

"The Tin Man"_____

"The Scarecrow"_____

"The Lion"_____

"Dorothy"_____

70

Where were you on November 22, 1963?

_____

Can you name...

The highest-rated police show in TV history?_____

The higest-rated, longest-running lawyer show in TV history?

_____

72

Can you sing the "Beverly Hillbillies" theme song?
Go ahead!

What do the words, "shag" and "olive green", mean to you?

_____

74

Who made their first appearance on "The Ed Sullivan Show", in February of 1964, while 68 million viewers tuned in?

_____

Who sang these songs?

"Takin' Care of Business"_____

"Takin' It To The Streets"_____

76

Remember these commercials?

"Shake and Bake® and I _____"

Everyone would be in love with you if you were what kind of hot dog?

_____

What did the "Frito®-Bandito" love?_____

What did astronauts drink?_____

Things Your Parents Said...

"When I was your _____, I walked 5 _____

to school in 6 feet of _____,

bare _____, up _____, both _____."

78

What was the name of the best-selling
"Fleetwood Mac" album?

_____

"Smile, You're On _____!"

80

Which TV show best describes the family you grew up in?

_____"The Munster's"   _____"The Little Rascals"

_____"The Twilight Zone"   _____"The Three Stooges"

_____None of the Above   _____All of the Above

Popular dance in the 70's.

"Funky_____"

82

"Sock it to me, sock it to me, sock it to me!"
What show?

_____

Who's "Herbie"?

_____

84

When did you get to move up from the "kids" table to the "adult" table at family holiday get-togethers?

_____

Name these TV Game Shows:

"My Name Is..."_____

"Circle Gets The Square..."_____

"Bachelor Number One..."_____

"Would You Sign In Please..."_____

86

What two circular "symbols" were popular in our era?
Draw them!

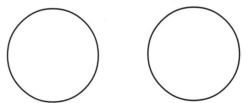

Name These Singers/Bands.

"Engelbert_____"

"Herb Alpert and the _____"

"Paul Revere and the_____"

"Herman's_____"

88

Can you sing your high school fight song?
Go ahead!

Remember these TV shows?

What is "black gold" and "texas tea?"_____

Who had "hair of gold" like their mother?_____

What kind of "time" did the Flintstones have?_____

Why was the "tiny ship" tossed?_____

Who said, "We're going to have a really big shoe!"?

_____

Name the popular men's suit of the 70's.

"Polyester_____"

92

Who were the two boys on "Flipper"?

_____   _____

What was the name of the popular "Doris Day" song?

_____

94

What did the "Wham-O Corporation®" first introduce in 1958?

_____

Remember this TV show?

Who were "Agent 86" and "Agent 99"?_____

What did "Agent 86" have in his shoe?_____

How did each episode of this show begin?_____

96

What was "long" and "beautiful" and "shining" and "gleamin'" and "steamin'" and "flaxin'" and "waxin'"?

_____

97

"One small step for man, one giant leap for mankind."
Who said that?

_____

98

"Book 'em, Dan-O!" What show?

_____

Name these popular male vocalists:

"Loggins & _____"

"Cat_____"

"Harry_____"

"Elton_____"

100

What is "Tiger Beat"?

_____

Who said, "Beep, Beep"?

_____

102

Name the "Lone Ranger's"...

Horse_____

Best Friend_____

Can you sing "The Brady Bunch" theme song?
Go ahead!

What did "Mr. Whipple" tell us not to squeeze?

_____Mrs. Whipple

_____The Charmin®

_____The Toothpaste

Name the 3 original "Charlie's Angels".

_____

_____

_____

106

What did "Jim Croce" want to save in a bottle?

_____

In the 60's, thousands of people had a spiritual awakening, what was it called?

"_____ Movement"

108

How did every episode of these TV shows end?

"The Carol Burnett Show"_____

"The Walton's"_____

109

Remember these classics?

What did "Mary Poppins" say a spoon full of sugar would do?

_____

Who was the piano player on "Charlie Brown"? _____

Who would dream in her own little corner, in her own little room?

_____

What was the name of "Dorothy's" dog?_____

110

How many of these interior fashion trends did you grow up with?

_____Hanging Macrame Plant Holder

_____Beaded Room Divider

_____Red, Orange, or Harvest Gold Counter Tops

_____Foil-Like Wallpaper

Who were "Roseanne Roseanna Danna" and "Emily Patella"?

_____

112

Who sang these songs, "Go Away Little Girl",
"Sweet and Innocent", and "Yo-Yo"?

_____

Who were "James T. West" and "Artemus Gordon"?

_____

What would "self-destruct" in 5 seconds?

_____

Things your dad said...

"How would you like a _____ sandwich?"

"You're cruisin'_____."

"Do you want me to stop this car and _____."

Name these popular male and female vocalists...

Who sang, "When Will I Be Loved?" and "That'll Be The Day"?

_____

Who sang, "You've Got a Friend" and "Fire and Rain"?

_____

Remember the "Drive-In Movie Theatre"?

What happened if you tried to enter in at the exit?

_____

How many people could you fit in your trunk?

_____

118

Who was "Archie's" girlfriend?

_____Betty

_____Veronica

Who sang these songs?

"Stayin' Alive"_____

"Up, Up and Away"_____

"Knock Three Times"_____

120

Name these cartoons.

"Mighty_____"

"Under_____"

"Scooby_____"

"Lippy The Lion And _____"

"George Of_____"

These characters were on what TV shows?

"Adam", "Hoss" and "Little Joe"_____

"Festus" and "Miss Kitty"_____

122

Remember this commercial?
"You can't buy them, you can only get them in boxes of "Breeze!"
What?

_____

"Mr. Spock" of "Star Trek" fame was...

Part "Human" and Part "_____"

Who was the star of "That Girl"?

_____

Remember these food and drink items?

"Space Food_____"

"Bonomo Turkish_____"

"_____ Crush®"

Describe the classic "Saturday Night Fever" disco outfit? Did you have one?

Fabric_____

Color_____

Lapels_____

Who sang these songs?

"Close To You"_____

"Feelings"_____

"Saturday, In The Park"_____

128

Finish these TV Show Titles.

"Man From_____"

"I Dream_____"

"The Bionic_____"

What used to be included in the trading card package?
(Hint: Baseball Cards, Batman Cards, Beatles Cards...)

_____

130

Remember these characters?

"Bullwinkle" and "_____"

"Yoggi Bear" and "_____" too!

"Gumby®" and "_____"

"Tom Terrific and His Mighty Dog_____"

"The Sounds of Silence" and "Bridge Over Troubled Water"
Who sang these?

_____

132

What 3 assassinations took place in our childhood?

_____

_____

_____

Who are "Monty Hall" and "Carol Merrill"?

_____

134

When we were kids, what kind of candy could we buy for a penny?

_____

Who said...
"My name is Edith Ann, and I am five years old..."

_____

What was the "van" of choice in our childhood?

_____

What is "Woodstock"?

_____A bird in the "Peanuts®" cartoon.

_____A gathering of 1000's of disillusioned young
        people in Bethel, New York in August of 1969?

_____Both of the above

138

Which word describes your teen years?

_____"Groovy"   _____"Bogue"

_____"Peace"   _____"Heavy"

_____"Love"   _____"Bomb"

_____"Cool"   _____"Hip"

Name these TV Shows.

"Welcome Back_____"

"McHale's_____"

"Please Don't Eat_____"

"The Six Million_____"

140

According to the TV show theme song,
what kind of man was "Daniel Boone"?

_____

"Flower_____"

Do you remember what those little flower decals were called?

_____

142

Name at least 2 "Barbra Streisand" movies you saw as a kid.

_____

_____

Name two detective TV shows from our era.

_____

_____

Who sang, "I Got You Babe"?

_____

Who were the "Honeymooners"? Name them.

_____   _____

_____   _____

Perfumes of our era, "Cachet", "Ambush"...

"Wind_____"

"Jean_____"

"Old_____"

Who is "Little Ricky"?

_____

148

Remember the "Name Game" song?
Can you sing it with your name?
(Hint..."Debbie, Debbie..." or "Steve, Steve...", or your name!)

More things your mother said...

"Do you think I don't have anything else to do but_____?"

You said, "Tommy's mom said he could..."
Your mom said, "Well, I'm_____!"

You said, "Mom, everyone's doing it..."
Your mom said, "If everyone jumped_____"

You said, "Mom, why do I have to do that...or why can't I do that... "
Your mom said, "Because I _____"

150

Finally, remember this "matchmaking" scenario?
You are the "messenger" and you say, "Johnny do you like Michelle?" He replies, "Does she like me?" You say, "If you like her, she likes you." He responds by buying Michelle an "ID bracelet" and asking her if she wants to "go steady". They never have another conversation, and technically 25 years later, they are still "going together." What grade were you in when this scene took place?

_____

CORRECT ANSWERS.

Put an "X" in the blank space if you got all or part a multiple choice question correct!

1. _____ Bell Bottoms and Hip Huggers! (Remember Elephant & Whale Bells? How about home-made "rip the side seam & insert fabric" bells...and we thought those were so cool!)

2. _____ Donny Osmond; Davey Jones; Bobby Sherman; David Cassidy

3. _____ "Close the door, were you born in a barn?"; "If you think it's my job to pick up after you, you've got another thing coming!"; "Eat your food there are children starving in India"; "Your room looks like a pig sty! or a tornado hit it!" (Universal sayings...where do mother's get these? How many of these have you said?)

4. _____ Monkees

5. _____ A 3 hour tour

6. _____ Jane, his wife; boy, Elroy; daughter, Judy; ...and of course, Astro ('Rastro)

7. _____ Tennis Shoes (You could run faster and jump higher remember?)

8. _____ The Robot on Lost in Space

9. _____ Burger King®; The Pepsi® Generation; A Break Today; To Sing

10. _____ Buffy's doll, from the TV show Family Affair

11. _____ Hoola Hoop®; Platform Shoes; Mood Ring; Lava Lamp®; Pet Rock; Pooca Beads

12. _____ We trust you! Take the point!

13. _____ Sam I Am (Didn't you love that book? in a nook? with a hook?)

14. _____ Carol, Mike, Marsha, Jan, Cindy, Greg, Peter, Bobby (and of course, Alice!)

15. _____ Stairway To Heaven

16. _____ Uncle Bill; Sissy; Mr. French

17. _____ Cooties were germs of the opposite sex and the spray was invisible protection from those germs! (Remember the "Cootie Catcher's" we made by folding a piece of square paper in various ways into four sections?)

18. _____ Fred Flintstone (and his lovely wife Wilma, daughter Pebbles and pet Dino, in the great town of Bedrock!)

19. _____ Captain Jean Luc Picard (Who?)

20. _____ To ride on the back wheel of a bike, while the front wheel is raised up in the air - the longer the better!

21. _____ Linc; Pete; Julie

22. _____ The Partridge Family

23. _____ Watched The Wonderful World of Disney! (On a really special night we had McDonald's® and Jiffy Pop®!)

24. _____ Rob and Laura Petri and their son, Richie

25. _____ We trust you...take the point!

26. _____ Characters from the game Clue®

27. _____ Batman (The Caped Crusader and The Boy Wonder!)

28. _____ Michael, Tito, Jermaine, Marlon and Jackie

29. _____ Romper Room (Did she ever say your name?)

30. _____ The Poseidon Adventure; The Towering Inferno; Jaws; Rocky

31. _____ Beaver Cleaver's brother and his brother's friend - ("Hello Mr. and Mrs. Cleaver. Hello Theodore")

32. _____ A Pixie was a short, little girls haircut that we disliked; A Bee Hive was a real tall "mom" hairdo; A Shag was the hair cut of the 70's!

33. _____ Hooterville

34. _____ One bad apple; A bullfrog; One is; Our house; My brother

35. _____ Put rubberbands all over various "wadded" sections of the t-shirt. Dip the shirt in your favorite color of Rit Dye. Rinse it out. Let it dry and remove all the rubberbands. Voila! (How about your jeans? Did you throw your jeans in a swimming pool to get them to fade?)

36. _____ You were in big trouble! The glare - tight lips, teeth clenched, finger pointed! The snap - loud and scary!

37. _____ We trust you! Take the point!

38. _____ Itsy, bitsy, teeny, weeny, yellow, polka-dot, bikini

39. _____ Walter Cronkite

40. _____ "Eace-pay and Ove-lay" Jibberish was where you put a "thg" sound after the first letter of each syllable!

41. _____ Go-Go Boots were tall, shiny, vinyl dance boots. Fish Net Nylons looked like fish nets and we thought they were cool! A Sizzler was a short, shiny, print dress with matching panties in the "Marsha Brady style."

42. _____ Marlin Perkins; Jim; Mutual of Omaha

43. _____ John Travolta; Olivia Newton-John

44. _____ We used clothes pins to put baseball cards, or other cards, on our bike near the spokes so they would make that "flutter" sound

45. _____ Characters on The Andy Griffith Show; Mayberry, North Carolina

46. _____ Shirley, Keith, Laurie, Danny, Chris, Tracy (and of course, Mr. Kincaid)

47. _____ Jefferson Airplane or Starship; Three Dog Night; The Moody Blues; Creedence Clearwater Revival

48. _____ Alfred E. Newman

49. _____ We trust you! Take a point!

50. _____ Hadji; Bandit

51. _____ You say, "Slug Bug" and you "slug" your neighbor on the arm (Was this just a girl thing?); Mini-Van

52. _____ Mr. Haney drove the junk truck; Arnold Ziffel was the famous pig

53. _____ The Beach Boys; Jan and Dean; Bob Dylan & Peter, Paul and Mary both sang "Blowin'"; The Kingston Trio

54. _____ Lovey

55. _____ Kick the Can; Einey-iney Over; Mother, May I?; Red Rover, Red Rover; Capture The Flag; Dodge Ball

56. _____ Love Story; If you love something you were supposed to let it go - remember?

57. _____ Gomer Pyle

58. _____ Gum; Chocolate Covered Sucker; Fizzy Candies

59. _____ Characters from Hogan's Heroes

60. _____ Orange

61. _____ Howdy Doody

62. _____ We trust you! Take the point.

63. _____ Stingray's were the coolest! Banana seats were the long seats, sissy bars were the tall bars on the back of the seat and were great for popping wheelies!

64. _____ Ernie, Chip, Robby

65. _____ Diana Ross and the Supremes; Helen Reddy; Carol King; Roberta Flack

66. _____ Ford Mustang (Can you believe it?)

67. _____ The Clampett's were worth $25 million; Jethro called a swimming pool a "cement pond"

68. _____ Olive Oil; Bruno

69. _____ Tin Man wanted a heart; Scarecrow wanted brains; Lion wanted courage; Dorothy wanted to go home

70. _____ That is the day that John F. Kennedy was assassinated

71. _____ Dragnet ("...the names have been changed to protect the innocent..."); Perry Mason

72. _____ We trust you! Take the point.

73. _____ Shag and Olive Green were the style and color of carpet in most every home in America!

74. _____ The Beatles

75. _____ Bachman, Turner, Overdrive - also know as BTO; The Doobie Brothers

76.	_____	Shake and Bake® and I Helped!; Oscar Meyer Weiner®; Frito's Corn Chips®; Tang®
77.	_____	"When I was your age, I walked 5 miles to school in 6 feet of snow, bare foot, up hill, both ways!" (Like we really believed them!)
78.	_____	Rumours
79.	_____	Candid Camera
80.	_____	Take the point! (Does this explain why some families are dysfunctional and co-dependent?)
81.	_____	Funky Chicken
82.	_____	Laugh In
83.	_____	The Love Bug
84.	_____	Wasn't that a great day? Take a point!
85.	_____	To Tell The Truth; Hollywood Squares; The Dating Game; What's My Line?
86.	_____	
87.	_____	Engelbert Humperdink; Herb Alpert and the Tijuana Brass; Paul Revere and the Raiders; Herman's Hermits
88.	_____	We trust you! Take the point.
89.	_____	Oil from The Beverly Hillbillies; The very lovely girls on The Brady Bunch; A yabba-dabba-do time; The weather started getting rough
90.	_____	Ed Sullivan
91.	_____	Polyester Leisure Suit

92. _____ Bud; Sandy

93. _____ Que Sera, Sera

94. _____ Hoola Hoop®

95. _____ Agent 86 (Maxwell Smart) and Agent 99 were characters on Get Smart; Maxwell Smart had a phone in his shoe; Each episode opened with them walking through a variety of opening doors

96. _____ Hair!

97. _____ Neil Armstrong

98. _____ Hawaii Five-O

99. _____ Loggins and Messina; Cat Stevens; Harry Chapin; Elton John

100. _____ Teen Magazine (It had all the scoop and great photo's of the teen stars!)

101. _____ The Roadrunner (How many times did the Coyote die?)

102. _____ Silver; Tonto

103. _____ We trust you! Take the point.

104. _____ The Charmin®

105. _____ Farah Fawcett; Kate Jackson; Jacqueline Smith

106. _____ Time

107. _____ Jesus Movement

108. _____ Carol Burnett pulled on her ear; The Walton's went through a "Goodnight John-Boy" exercise

109. _____ Sugar makes the medicine go down; Schroeder was the piano player; Cinderella; Toto

110. _____ Take the point! (How many hanging macrame plant holders did you have?)

111. _____ Characters played by Gilda Radner on Saturday Night Live

112. _____ Donny Osmond of course!

113. _____ The stars of The Wild, Wild West

114. _____ Cassette tape on the beginning of the show Mission Impossible

115. _____ "How would you like a knuckle sandwich?"; "You're cruisin' for a bruisin'"; "Do you want me to stop this car and turn around?, or give you a spanking?" Take a point!

116. _____ Linda Ronstadt; James Taylor

117. _____ Your tires were popped by the spikes; You didn't sneak people into the movie in your trunk did you?

118. _____ Veronica

119. _____ Bee Gees; The 5th Dimension; Tony Orlando and Dawn

120. _____ Mighty Mouse; Underdog; Scooby Doo; Lippy the Lion & Hardy Har-Har; George of the Jungle

121. _____ Bonanza; Gunsmoke

122. _____ Towels! (How much detergent did you really get when there was a big towel in the box?)

123. _____ Vulcan

124. _____ Marlo Thomas

125. _____ Space Food Sticks; Bonomo's Turkish Taffy; Orange Crush®

126. _____ Fabric was polyester; Color was white or powder blue; Lapels were huge

127. _____ The Carpenters; Morris Albert; Chicago

128. _____ Man from U.N.C.L.E.; I Dream of Jeannie; The Bionic Woman

129. _____ A piece of gum! (What ever happened to that piece of gum?)

130. _____ Rocky; Boo-Boo, Pokey®; Manfred (Remember this segment on Captain Kangaroo?)

131. _____ Simon and Garfunkel

132. _____ John F. Kennedy; Robert Kennedy; Martin Luther King

133. _____ The Host and Assistant of the game show, Let's Make a Deal

134. _____ Bit-O-Honey®; Bazooka Bubble Gum®; Shoestring Licorice, Lipstick, Wax Lips, plus more! Take the point!

135. _____ Lily Tomlin

136. _____ Volkswagen Bus

137. _____ Both

138. _____ Take the point!

139. _____ Welcome Back Kotter; McHale's Navy; Please Don't Eat the Daisies; The Six Million Dollar Man

140. _____ A big man!

141. _____ Flower Power or Flower Child; The flower decals were called Rickie Tickie Stickies

142. _____ The Way We Were; A Star Is Born; Funny Girl; What's Up Doc? - think of others? Take the point.

143. _____ Dragnet; Mannix; Columbo; Ironside; The Mod Squad and others - Take the point!

144. _____ Sonny and Cher

145. _____ Ralph, Alice, Ed and Trixie

146. _____ Windsong; Jean Nate; Old Spice

147. _____ Lucy and Desi's son on, I Love Lucy

148. _____ We trust you! Take the point!

149. _____ "Do you think I don't have anything else to do but pick up after you?"; "Well, I'm not Tommy's mom!"; "If everyone jumped off a bridge would you do it?"; "Because I said so!"

150. _____ 7th Grade! It was a Junior High thing!

Each Question Is Worth 1 Point.
Remember, this is not Master's Degree stuff! If you got at least half of a multiple choice question correct, take the point!

TOTAL NUMBER CORRECT:_____

SCORING:

SCORE: 0-50 - "Baby Boomer Wanna Be"
Okay, who are you and what do you want? Nice try! Good luck in the search to find your people!

SCORE: 51-150 - "Big Time, True Blue, Die Hard Baby Boomer"
Congratulations! You are one of us! You really did wear original bell bottoms!

ABOUT THE AUTHOR.

Looking ever so holy in 1967...

Beth Jones - I am a Baby Boomer, with fond memories of growing up in the 60's and 70's. One of my favorite thrills as a kid was the annual "school shopping trip" and the excitement of picking out clothes and a new lunch box. As a pre-teen, I remember how important it was to be a "cool" dancer, so I asked my little sister to teach me how to dance in go-go boots and fish-net nylons...well, let's just say it never seemed to click... and I got really tired of hearing "Venus" and "Build Me Up Buttercup"! In junior high and high school, hanging out with friends, watching TV, and listening to music were the "thing". Like most Baby Boomers my age, I absolutely loved "Donny Osmond", "The Monkees", "The Brady Bunch", "The Partridge Family," "The Beverly Hillbillies", "Petticoat Junction", and all the other fun TV shows we had back then...those were the days my friends, we thought they'd never end...hey, isn't that from our era too?

Today, in real life, I help my husband in pastoring a great church and I am the mother of four wonderful kids. (Technically, I think I'm a Soccer Mom.) I graduated from Boston University in 1981, went to Bible School, and now I spend most of my spare-time in ministry, helping people to experience God's best in their lives, through one-on-one meetings, public speaking, and writing. In addition to writing this "for-fun" book, I've written a series of three books, designed for Christian growth, *Getting A Grip On The Basics, Getting A Grip On Health and Healing,* and *Getting A Grip on Prosperous Living,* all published by Harrison House Publishers in Tulsa, Oklahoma.

Things are good in 1997...

BELL BOTTOM BOOKS ORDERING INFORMATION.

To order additional copies of **The Baby Boomer's Little Quiz Book**, please choose one of the following methods. (Also available - **The Soccer Mom's Little Quiz Book** - a fun book for every mom in America!)

#1:	Convenient Way:	Call your local bookstore to see if they carry our books. If not, bug them!
#2	Quickest Way:	Phone us at: **1-800-955-4077** to place your order with a credit card.
#3:	Slowest Way:	Mail us at: **P.O. Box 555, Richland, Michigan, 49083** to place your order. Make your check or money order payable to: **Bell Bottom Books**

Ship To - Name_____

Address_____

City/State/Zip_____

Day Phone_____

PLEASE
ALLOW 4-6
WEEKS FOR SHIPPING
•
VOLUME DISCOUNTS
AVAILABLE UPON REQUEST

HAVE IDEAS FOR VOLUME 2?
SUBMIT YOUR IDEAS TO THE
ADDRESS ON THIS PAGE.
IF YOUR IDEA IS USED IN A
FUTURE PUBLICATION YOUR
NAME WILL APPEAR ON A
VERY SPECIAL
ACKNOWLEDGMENTS
PAGE!

_____ Copies of "The Baby Boomer's Little Quiz Book" @ $9.95 ea. = $_____

_____ Copies of "The Soccer Mom's Little Quiz Book" @ $9.95 ea. = $_____

Postage & Handling @ $3.00 for 1 book $_____

Postage & Handling @ $1.00 per additional book- (Max. $10.00) $_____

Michigan Residents Add 6% tax $_____

Total Amount Enclosed $_____